THE *Sport Mites™*

S0-BRN-522

with FLUFFY SNOW and SPEEDY SLOPES in

SKI SCHOOL

Sport Mites ™ characters created
and drawn by Bob Pelkowski   Text by Alias Smith and Les Keller

BARRON'S
New York • London • Toronto • Sydney

ISBN 0-8120-4244-1
PRINTED IN HONG KONG

Sport Mite Fluffy Snow loves winter sports—especially skiing.
She came to play with her friend Sport Mite Speedy Slopes in
his yard.

"Speedy, you look sad," Fluffy said.

"My sled is broken," Speedy said. "It won't be fixed until
tomorrow, and you know how I like sledding."

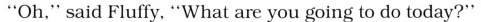

"Oh," said Fluffy, "What are you going to do today?"

"Go inside and wait for tomorrow," Speedy said sadly.

"I've got a better idea," Fluffy said. "Can you ski?"

"I've never tried," Speedy answered.

"Let's go to the Mitey Clubhouse, and I'll show you how," Fluffy said with a big smile.

On the way they stopped at Fluffy's house to get her skis, poles, and boots, and to ask her brother if Speedy could use his equipment—which all fit like magic.

Speedy promised to take good care of everything, and they headed for the Mitey Clubhouse.

The Mitey Clubhouse is the special place where all the Sport Mites adventures take place. As they came to the Mitey Clubhouse, Redbert, the trusted friend and mascot of all the Sport Mites, stopped shoveling the snow and greeted them. "I see you've come to ski on the hill behind the Clubhouse," he said excitedly.

Fluffy asked Redbert, "Will you help me teach Speedy how to ski?"

Redbert proudly answered, "Sure. We can pretend we are at Ski School. I'll hang this sign on the clubhouse door and make it official."

Redbert can usually help the Sport Mites with just about anything.

As Fluffy and Speedy sat down, Fluffy said, "Watch how I put on my ski boots."

Redbert watched, too. He made sure the boot buckles were on the outside of the ankles on each foot.

Speedy stood up and said, "These boots are heavy and won't let me bend my feet."

"Yes," said Fluffy. "But you can still walk in them. Watch me walk like a soldier. Heel . . . toe! Heel . . . toe!"

They marched around in the snow for a while, until Redbert said, "I thought you wanted to ski down the hill."

"That's right, I almost forgot," Speedy admitted.

Fluffy said, "Let's march over to the hill and get started."

"Your ski boots are full of snow. You'll have to kick the snow off before you put on your skis," Redbert reminded Fluffy.

Then Fluffy showed Speedy how to place the boot toe into the toe piece and the boot heel into the heel piece of the ski.

"Like this?" Speedy asked.

"Yes," answered Fluffy. "Push down on the heel and listen for the click."

Redbert said, "Fluffy, can you show Speedy how to side-step up a hill with skis on? He has to be able to get up the hill before he can learn to ski down it."

"Sure I can. Watch me," she said. Fluffy began by lifting one foot and stepping to the side, keeping the ski pointing in the same direction that it was before. When the ski was again firmly in place on the snow, she lifted the other foot and put it down next to the first foot. Fluffy said, "Always keep the skis pointing in the same direction and don't put one ski on top of the other one."

After a little practice at the bottom of the hill, Fluffy said, "Let's side-step up the hill. I'll go first and you can follow."

Speedy thought this was fun and couldn't wait to get to the top of the small hill.

At the top of the hill Speedy said, "I'm ready now. I want to go down the hill."

"Just a minute," Fluffy yelled. "You need to know how to keep your balance. Just hold the ends of the ski poles, one in each hand, and bend your knees like this and skiing will be easier."

"Let's pretend we're riding a scooter down the hill. Bend your knees and follow me," Fluffy said as she pushed off with the ski poles and started down.

    Speedy anxiously followed her down the hill. As he glided to a slow stop at the bottom of the hill, he said, "I didn't even fall down or stop with a crash . . . this is fun."

    Redbert was waiting at the bottom of the hill for them. "That's great," Redbert said. "Do you think you can do that again?"

Speedy and Fluffy practiced side-stepping up the hill and skiing down the hill many more times.

Then, Redbert flew to them at the top of the hill and asked, "Have you figured out how to control your speed as you come down yet?"

Fluffy remembered what she learned last year and said, "I know how to go fast and slow down the hill."

Speedy said, "I can go fast, but how do you go slow?"

Fluffy answered, "Point your toes toward each other and push out your heels. The more you push your heels out the slower you go."

Redbert said, "That's right, Fluffy. It's easy to remember if you think of a piece of pizza when you point your skis. The smaller the piece of pizza, the faster you go. The fatter the piece, the slower you go."

Speedy said, "I want to go down the hill fast, but slow down at the bottom, without using a flat area to help. Watch me!" And he started down the hill again, this time with more courage than before.

Fluffy and Redbert watched Speedy ski down the hill.
Near the bottom of the hill Speedy yelled, ''Pizza delivery
man,'' as he pushed out his heels and came to a smooth stop.

Redbert and Fluffy followed and met Speedy at the bottom of the hill. Speedy said, "Ski School is great."

Redbert asked, "Do you know what a rope tow is?"

Speedy said, "A rope . . . what?"

Fluffy smiled knowingly and said, "I know. A rope tow is a moving rope that pulls you up from the bottom to the top of a BIG hill."

Speedy asked, "Can we make one?"

Fluffy answered, "Sure we can. All we need is a long rope, and we can get one at the Mitey Clubhouse."

After getting the rope, Fluffy asked Redbert to fly one end of the long rope to the top of the BIG hill and tie it to a BIG tree.

"We can tie the other end to a BIG tree at the bottom of the hill," Fluffy said as she and Speedy pulled the rope tightly between the trees.

Fluffy said, "This can be our rope tow to help us get up the BIG hill, but this rope doesn't move. We'll have to pull ourselves along using the rope to help us."

"That's okay," Speedy said, "Let's give it a try."

Speedy said, "This hill is much higher than the first hill we were on. This rope tow is a big help."

Fluffy agreed as they pulled themselves up the BIG hill.

Fluffy said, "We finally made it to the top of this hill. Look how high up we are."

Speedy thought, "I know I can go 'Speedy' fast down the hill and slow down without crashing . . . I remember the pizza lesson." Then Speedy grinned a big smile and said, "This really is a BIG hill."

Fluffy said, "Since this is your first time going down a BIG hill, let's go together. We can pretend we are a train. I'll be the engine and you can be the caboose."

Speedy thought that was a great idea, and they started down the hill.

They each were shouting, "Choo-Choo" as they chugged on all the way to the bottom.

Redbert watched proudly as his ski friends enjoyed pulling themselves up and skiing down the BIG hill.

"Skiing is so much fun," Speedy said to Fluffy. "Thanks for showing me how to do it."

Speedy and Fluffy enjoyed hours of skiing fun together. Speedy even learned how to make a wide letter "S" in the snow as he practiced skiing down the hill.

At the end of the afternoon, Redbert called to Fluffy and Speedy, "Come over here. I have something for both of you."

"You learned a lot about skiing and playing together today," Redbert said. "You each have earned a Sport Mites ski badge." As Redbert pinned the shiny badges onto their outfits, he said, "This badge means that you know the basics about skiing, that you are safe and careful skiers, and that you are willing to help others. Congratulations!"

Speedy said, "If we keep practicing, do you think maybe, someday, someone can take us to a really big ski hill?"

Redbert smiled and said, "Keep practicing and I'm sure that will happen."

Speedy and Fluffy took off the skis and ski boots and headed home.

Speedy said, "I'm going to clean your brother's skis, poles, and boots so they're just like they were when he lent them to me . . . clean, dry, and shiny. Then maybe he'll let me practice skiing with them again."

SKIING TERMS

ski boots   Special stiff boots made to be clamped into skis.

ski   A long, narrow strip of wood or fiberglass attached under each ski boot for gliding over snow.

ski poles   A pair of tubes made of wood, fiberglass or metal, each with a handle and a strap at the top, and a pointed metal tip at the bottom, used to help a skier glide over snow.

rope tow   A rope that pulls skiers up a hill; usually a motor is used to pull the rope along.

slope   A snow-covered hill.

side-step   A way to walk sideways up a slope.

ski school   A special school, usually on big slopes, where kids and adults can learn how to ski.

EQUIPMENT TIPS

Ski equipment, like all sport equipment, should be properly taken care of so that the equipment will remain in good working condition.

Ski equipment needs to be dried off after use, because the snow that gets on the equipment will melt and become water. Leaving water on certain types of equipment could cause it to rust, warp, or discolor.

Skis need to be waxed to make them slippery. This helps them glide over the snow and makes skiing easier.

Ski equipment should be stored in a safe place where it won't get broken by accident. The storage place should be clean and neat.

Skiing can be fun and exciting, but like any sport, accidents can happen. You need to learn how to use the ski equipment properly, and practice carefully.

SAFETY TIP
LEARN TO IDENTIFY THE SKI SLOPE MARKERS

MARKER	DESCRIPTION

Bunny Hill Marker

The Bunny Hill Marker identifies a slope for children and first time skiers. The slope is very gradual with no difficulty. This is the smallest of the ski hills.

Green Marker

The Green Marker identifies the beginner slope for new skiers. This slope is gradual and long, but more difficult than the Bunny Hill.

Blue Marker

The Blue Marker identifies the intermediate slope for skiers with experience. The slope is more difficult and more steep than a beginner slope.

Black Marker

The Black Marker identifies the expert slope for skiers with expert ski skills and experience. The slope is the most difficult and most steep of all ski hills.

At all ski resorts, the ski slopes are marked by colored signs. These signs may vary in size and shape, but in most cases, the colors are universal. Bunny Hills are always identified with the words ''Bunny Hill'' printed on the marker. Before you ski on a resort slope, ask the ski instructor how the slopes are marked at the resort.